HEARING THE HOLY

Restoring the Devotional Reading of Scripture

Bryan Nash

Hearing the Holy: Restoring the Devotional Reading of Scripture
© 2017 by DeWard Publishing Company, Ltd.
P.O. Box 6259, Chillicothe, Ohio 45601
800.300.9778
www.deward.com

Cover design by Evangela Creative.

Printed in the United States of America.

ISBN: 978-1-947929-01-2

Table of Contents

Introduction

"She reads the Bible but she doesn't really study it." I can still hear the crackling voice of the older lady as she spoke about a friend of hers who lived over the hill. It was said in a less than congratulatory way. As if to say that there are those uninformed folks who just pick up the Bible and read it, and then there are those who really get into the meat—they study. I've heard similar things said about churches. "Those folks at the church up the road with the funny name just read the Bible. In here, we study it."

Imagine two people for a moment. The first sits next to the dancing flame of the fireplace with the Scriptures in her lap and a cup of tea in her shaky hand. Knowing that most any Psalm will provide a chance to hear the voice of God, she opens her well-worn Bible at its center (always a good way to find the Psalms). As the antique binding stretches and an old recipe falls out, the page lands on Psalm 120. Through dim eyes she reads, "In my distress I called to the LORD and he answered me."

She stops. She closes the book and she closes her eyes. She lets the words that she just read flow over her. She knows distress. Brittle bones and hard of hearing, she knows distress.

She knows what it is like to be looked at with contempt and she knows the regret of having looked at others with contempt. She remembers the stress of having to find a way to put food on the table and clothes on the kid's backs when her husband wasn't around. Her arthritic fingers remember making clothes that the children would be proud of. Yes, she knows distress.

And she knows that in her distress, God answered. They didn't have a surplus but they always had plenty. "In my distress I called to the LORD, and he answered me," she says to herself, reciting the Psalm. Surrounded by the warmth of God that surpasses the warmth of the fire, she prays, "Thank you, God, for answering me in my distress." She finishes her tea, takes care of the fireplace, and goes to bed.

On the other side of town, a young man is preparing to lead a Bible study. Fresh out of Bible college, he can parse Greek verbs with the best of them. He lays out his commentaries, gets out his maps of the ancient world, and fires up his laptop just in case he needs to search some academic journals. He's ready to go. With coloring pencils representing every color of the rainbow, he begins to studiously doodle on the page. Highlights, circles, stars, arrows—an artistic ensemble that would make the most gifted artist proud.

With carefully constructed notes in one hand and a thesaurus in the other, he devises a three-point outline. It is even alliterated so that each point flows off of the tongue, making it easy to remember. He closes the Bible, checks some emails, and goes to bed.

One person just read. The other studied. Which is better?

As is the case with most things, we tend to artificially create two categories and then pit these artificially created cat-

egories against each other. When we do so, we end up thinking that one is better than the other. My purpose here is not
to chart the history of how people have approached the Bible. For my purposes, it will suffice to say that over the years,
many people came to look down on our lady by the fire and
exalt our lad in front of the laptop.

With this book, I am calling for restoration. I am calling for a restoration of the devotional reading of Scripture
in our churches. Most of us today read Scripture on a phone
or on a tablet that is equipped with commentaries, concor-
dances, Greek and Hebrew resources, etc. We also have inter-
net access at the touch of a button if our study program isn't
enough. Things were much different just a few generations
ago. In short, many people today read Scripture hoping to
get some good information. I've even heard Bible class teach-
ers says things like, "Tonight, I've got some good facts for us."
Or, "We've got a lot of information to cover. Let's get started." Sometimes this information takes the form of places and
dates, other times it takes the form of better money manage-
ment or better parenting. But at the heart, we read because we
want some good information.

Once upon a time, people did not read Scripture so much
for information. They read wanting formation. They wanted
to hear a word from the Holy One. When the pages were
opened it was believed that they were about to hear the Holy.
It was a kind of reading that truly expected a very real encounter to occur.

Many books have been published trying to teach us how to
be like our young man in the scenario above. Sometimes local
churches even get in on the action. We offer classes teaching

people to diagram sentences, learn beginning Greek and Hebrew, and read commentaries. Of course, these classes are only for our more "advanced students" in the church. What I wish to propose is that, if we're busy learning to distinguish nominative singular nouns from accusative plural nouns in hopes of growing closer to God, there might be an elderly lady sitting next to a fireplace somewhere who could teach us a lot.

This book is divided into two parts. Certain aspects of this material might seem a bit unorthodox to some, so I might as well continue this trend in the introduction—allow me to introduce Part Two before introducing Part One. Part Two of the book proposes a way of reading Scripture as a devotional/journaling practice. I have led a few men's retreats at my congregation. In looking for material to be used at these events, I have realized that there are very few books that help people to engage the Bible devotionally. There are many books that can help us study the Bible with the intellect. Also, there are many "devotionals" that encourage a person to read a nice thought from the author of the book every day. There are fewer books, however, that help one hear a living word from the Author of the Book. Part Two provides an approach that, hopefully, fills this void and promotes a deeper spirituality and sense of God's presence in one's life.

Now, let's talk about Part One. Part One is intended to provide the Scriptural foundation for the journaling approach in Part Two. I developed this material for use at my own congregation, and I've presented some of the content at other churches as well. People have been very supportive of the material. Their encouragement has helped me to stay the course in shaping the content into chapters and making these chapters available to others. I especially want to thank the King Street Church of Christ in Beaufort, South Carolina.

Allow me to make one more quick observation at the outset. Sometimes I might speak a bit tongue-in-cheek when it comes to academic, intellectual approaches to Scripture. Please hear those portions correctly. Some of my closest friends are academics and I've contributed to some published academic works. So, my criticism is not against academics or even academic approaches. My discontent is with those who fail to realize that, in most cases, a devotional approach to reading the Bible will do far more for our spiritual growth than something that gets labeled "deep" or "meaty." At least, I know this to be true in my own life.

Part One

It's Alive

"For the word of God is living and active, sharper than any two-edged sword, piercing to the division of soul and of spirit, of joints and of marrow, and discerning the thoughts and intentions of the heart." Hebrews 4.12

One of the most memorable scenes in the history of cheesy horror films came in the 1931 rendition of Frankenstein. A young scientist named Victor Frankenstein creates a monster from the parts of corpses. When the monster begins to move on the table, Victor exclaims, almost in a surprised way, "It's alive! It's alive!"

For the last century or so people have created a Frankenstein approach to Scripture. Rather than being viewed as a coherent story of God's work in the world, Scripture has come to be viewed as a lifeless, pieced together thing. This became the case in the university, but it has also trickled into the church. Most Christians don't realize the extent to which they've been influenced by the Frankenstein approach.

With little thought given to prayer and God's involvement, we put the text on the table and get out our tools that will help to create the monster that is our interpretation—commentaries, encyclopedias, maps, and maybe even an old outline or two. And yet in spite of all our efforts, the text continues to lie there on the table. Lifeless. Cold. Pale. No wonder many people get burned out on the idea of Bible study.

Then one day it happens. It has happened to most Christians at some point. We pick up the Bible and read it—maybe just a verse or two—and suddenly that lifeless, cold, pale text seems as though it is moving on the table. These words have laid bare our secrets and given us hope in our sorrow. "It's alive!" is the only thing we can say. And I believe this is what God wants us to say as we encounter God in Holy Scripture. Or perhaps more precisely we ought to say, "God's alive!" If God is alive, then in a sense, so are the words from God.

Hebrews says that "the word of God is living and active, sharper than any two-edged sword, piercing to the division of soul and of spirit, of joints and of marrow, and discerning the thoughts and intentions of the heart" (Heb 4.12). This verse is dealing with more than just the words on the pages of our Bibles. And it's dealing with more than Christ, who "was the Word" (Jn 1.1). In Scripture we encounter God. We have words that have gone out which will not return to Him empty (Is 55.11).

It's alive! Obviously, it is not alive in a literal, biological sense. You can't take Scripture's blood pressure or check its pulse. But somehow, the text we hold in our hands is alive. And the only way to really get to know something that is alive is to spend time with it. There is no substitute.

Living things are unpredictable. While there might be some patterns to their behavior, living things will surprise and shock you. Sometimes they will challenge you and even bite you. So it is with our reading of Scripture. If it is truly alive, then to open the pages is to enter into a risky situation. Just when we think we've tamed the text and put it in a cage, it breaks loose. This living thing can't be imposed upon. It can't be contained by our expectations. If it hasn't yet, it will get up off the table and break the chains we've laid across it. It's alive.

Not only is it living, but it is also active. Things that are active like to keep moving. They stay busy. They don't just sit still. They are always going somewhere and doing something. I'm afraid we often think of ourselves as the living and active ones who are approaching the lifeless words of God. Somehow we must make these lifeless words interesting, we think. Yet as much as we like to believe that we are in control, this living and active word will impose its will on us if we are open to the possibility. It does things. It comforts. It convicts. It creates realities that we didn't know were possible. It's alive.

It's like a sword that can cut deep. It's not a dull blade but rather it is sharper than any sword we might imagine. It cuts right to the heart. It even knows what we're thinking. It discerns our thoughts and intentions. I don't know about you, but to me, that sounds a little scary. I thought I was just reading a book. But really, I'm picking up something that can discern my thoughts and my intentions. When God's words go out, they do what God Himself does. It's alive.

Another portion of Scripture that is helpful in thinking about the living words of God is 2 Timothy 3.14–17. "But as for you, continue in what you have learned and have firmly believed, knowing from whom you learned it and how from childhood you have been acquainted with the sacred writings, which are able to make you wise for salvation through faith in Christ Jesus. All Scripture is breathed out by God and profitable for teaching, for reproof, for correction, and for training in righteousness, that the man of God may be complete, equipped for every good work."

These verses often serve as the battleground for debates on theories of inspiration. Some translators have translated the Greek word *theopneustos* as "inspired by God," while others think "God-breathed" is a better translation. Without getting into the nitty-gritty details, it will suffice to say that we really don't know what this word means. Translators can just make an educated guess. So, it's quite interesting that debates about "inspiration" have been had over a word with an unsure meaning. At the end of the day, I think this verse has as much to do with the function of Scripture as it does the origin of Scripture. It doesn't tell us precisely how it is that Scripture is Scripture. Rather, it tells us what the Scriptures accomplish. They teach, reprove, correct, and train in righteousness. They equip us and make us complete.

Scripture is here described as *doing* something. It's alive. While these verses might be used to put together a theory of how "inspiration" happened ages ago, we would do well to think about what Scripture is doing presently. When read alongside Hebrews 4.12, perhaps the best way of reading this verse is to conclude that God is encountered in Scripture. Through the Scriptures, God breathes life into the church, life into our homes, and life into our daily tasks. The Scriptures originate with God, but He has not quit breathing life into death through His words that have gone out.

Thinking of Scripture as a living and active word from God makes me arrive at this question: How would I approach the Bible differently if I thought that it was actually capable of doing something? In our speech, we usually convey the idea that we do something to the Bible. We study it, memorize it, teach it, and highlight it. We might even be inclined to talk about what we can do to others with the Bible. Mainly, we can chastise them and point out their faults.

Perhaps you've had a different experience, but we tend to not be as inclined to speak of what Scripture is doing to us. There is a self-surrender that must occur. In a sense, only after Scripture has studied me can I study it. Only after it has taught me can I feebly attempt to teach it to others. Only after it has highlighted my faults and frailty can I get out my yellow marker and go to town.

If I really thought that these living words could do something to me, I wonder if I would approach them with more reverence. I think it is great that Scripture is available in so many formats today. Phones, tablets, laptops...if it's electronic you can probably figure out a way to put a Bible app on it. Yet the reality is, we oftentimes fail to appreciate the things that are easy to get. I seldom truly thank God for my daily food like I should. After all, I don't typically worry about whether or not I will have three meals. I could have four or five if I wanted. I don't thank Him for water like I should. All I have to do is turn the faucet on. I'm worried that perhaps we don't thank Him for His words like we should. All we have to do is turn on the phone and there they are, right next to the weather forecast and current events. We would do well to adopt the position of the people in Ezra. When Ezra opened the book, everybody stood (Ez 8.5). They didn't stand because they needed to stretch their legs before a long sermon, they stood because they knew that when the book was opened, God was being encountered. You don't slouch when you come before the King.

If I really thought that these living words could do something to me, I wonder if I would approach them more slowly and more carefully. There is a time to read fast and cover a lot of ground, but there is also a time to read slowly, allowing the words adequate time to cover me. We tend to do the former better than the latter. We feel good about ourselves if we get through the Bible in a year. Maybe we even feel like we have mastered the text. But in reading all of those words, have we allowed the text to master us? Have we let it seep into the darkest corners of our lives? Have we encountered the living and active words or have we simply read a bunch of words written long ago?

How might I approach Scripture differently if I really believed that through those active and living words, God could breathe new life into my situation? I might just put this book down and pick up the Book that contains those words. But beware, it's alive.

Come to the Feast

"Make me understand the way of your precepts, and I will medi-tate on your wondrous works." Psalm 119.27

What images come to mind when you hear the word *medi-tate?* Perhaps some think of a Buddhist with legs crossed and eyes closed. He's meditating. Maybe others think of some-thing like a yoga class—breathing, stretching, meditating. Whatever it is you might think of, reading Scripture prob-ably isn't the first thing that comes to mind when you hear the word *meditate.*

We tend not to associate the words *meditate* and Scrip-ture. Eastern religions and meditation—well, that goes to-gether. The mind/body connection and meditation—that works. Time spent with nature and meditation—that could be, too. But Scripture and meditation—hmm, that doesn't sound quite right.

Despite our initial discomfort with the idea, the Old Tes-tament frequently speaks of the need to meditate on God and God's words. This is especially the case in the Psalms. The Psalms speak of meditating on the delightful words of God throughout the day (Ps 1.2), meditating on God in the evening when it is time for bed (Pss 63.6; 119.148), meditating on the works of God (Pss 77.12; 143.5), meditating on the commandments of God (Ps 119.15, 48, 78), and meditating amidst difficulties (Ps 119.23).

So, what does Scripture mean by *meditate?* I think two verses in particular are helpful as we begin to think about this. In Genesis 24.63 it says that "Isaac went out to meditate in the field toward evening." Isaac isn't going to a party. He's going to the field to be alone. But not totally alone. He's probably going to the field to be with God.

A second verse that is helpful is Psalm 119.27. The writer prays, "Make me understand the way of your precepts, and I will meditate on your wondrous works." Understanding and meditating are seen as two separate activities. Once there is understanding, then there is to be a period of meditating.

There are a couple of Hebrew words that are translated *meditate* or *meditation* in our Bibles. They are connected to the idea of uttering something. It could be that meditation involves talking to yourself, or talking inwardly, about God and God's words. They say that you're not crazy if you talk to yourself, only if you answer. But it may be that meditation is just that—it's the conversation that you have with yourself as you think about Scripture. It could be out loud, but it could also be silent. This seems to be the sense at times. One of the Psalms says, "Let me remember my song in the night, let me meditate in my heart" (Ps 77.6).

Or, it could be that meditate or meditation is simply another way of speaking about prayer. It certainly is closely connected. For example, David says in Psalm 143 that he will meditate on what God has done. After this he writes, "I stretch out my hands to you" (Ps 143.6).

But it could also be the case that meditation involves talking to others. It doesn't have to be done in isolation. Many of the Psalms connect meditation with speaking or singing (Pss 19.14; 49.3; 104.33–34).

However it is that we want to define meditation, ultimately it seems to be kind of like eating. The normal way to eat is to put food into your mouth and then chew it for a little while. After you've chewed on it sufficiently, you swallow. Then, the food starts working for you. But we all tend to be in a hurry. If you eat too fast you might even choke. I remember reading somewhere that you are supposed to chew your food about 30 times before swallowing. The next time you eat, count how many times you chew before you swallow. It's probably not 30. We are in a hurry. Seldom do we even slow down to enjoy a meal.

I can recall being out to eat one time and some of the people were picking on someone for eating slowly. He said, "Well, I just like to taste my food before I swallow it." Essentially, that's what meditating on the Scriptures is like. It is slowing down to taste the Scriptures.

Chefs will tell you that a good meal involves all the senses. The presentation involves sight. The vibrant colors of the carefully arranged food is a feast for the eyes. Scent is equally important. How many times have you said this before a meal? "Ohh, it smells good." Before we eat it, we smell it. Sometimes, we even hear it. Mexican-food lovers enjoy listening to the sizzle of the fajitas. Having used the eyes and the nose, we then either pick it up or use silverware. Even the utensils are important. It's hard to enjoy a good meal if you have a crooked spoon or a knife that won't cut. Finally, the food comes to your mouth. Ice-cream connoisseurs have a particular way of putting the ice cream on the tongue. This is not just food, it's an experience!

Reading Scripture is like going to a fine restaurant. It ought to be a feast that involves all the senses. For example, as we read the story of Jesus cleansing the temple, how do we go about it? Do you take the time to watch Jesus fashion a whip, his nimble fingers working the cords? Do you take the time to smell the oxen and the sheep and the doves? Can you hear the clank of the coins and the crashing of the tables? Do we take the time to step into the story, or do we give it a speedread and then put it down, never thinking about it again?

Even if we spend time with a story, we may not really be taking the time to chew on it. Oftentimes, "deep" Bible study consists of looking up Greek words, checking cross-references, and reading encyclopedias. And, for good measure, we may come up with an application "for your everyday life," as they say. Then, when all is done, the books are closed. Bible study is over. On to something else.

Even though we have spent some time with it, we haven't chewed on it. We may have even choked on the words because we tried to swallow them so quickly. We haven't stepped into the story and been changed. We've just improved our ability to flip through books. Maybe this is an overstatement, but oftentimes we treat Scripture more like a fast food drive-thru and less like a fine dining experience. If it is a place we haven't been before, we take a minute to look over the menu. If it is a place that we frequent often, we get the same old burger we always get and speed away, scarfing it down while listening to the radio and criticizing other drivers. This isn't really a meal that you enjoy. It just puts something in your stomach. But even at that, what you have put in your stomach probably isn't of a very good quality.

Ultimately, by reading meditatively, and continuing to meditate on what we have read, we are spending time with God in Scripture. Too often, as we open the Book, we use it as a way of reflecting on current events. Or, we might use it as a way of convincing ourselves that the person in the pew in front of us is wrong. Or, we might use it as a way of condemning the church up the road.

But God did not author Scripture primarily so that we could have help in deciding whether to vote Republican or Democrat. He did not author Scripture so that we might feel superior to others. And while it is true that Scripture gives us doctrine and authority for our practices, those things flow out of a relationship with God. I do believe we find propositions in Scripture which are to be upheld, but those propositions stem from our relationship with a living God—a God who is encountered in Holy Scripture. Without a relationship, "doctrine" becomes nothing more than a series of loosely connected, lifeless statements.

Open the Book and enjoy the feast that is before you. Come to the table prepared for the finest meal of your life. Behold the beauty of the arrangement. Smell the succulent aromas filling the room. Chew it slowly, enjoying the robust flavors.

Open the Book. Read it. Meditate on it. Come, and taste and see that the Lord is good.

Learning to Listen

"If one gives an answer before he hears, it is his folly and shame."
Proverbs 18.13

We've all heard that we have two ears and one mouth for a reason. We ought to listen more than we speak. Ironically, this saying seems to have originated with a philosopher. Philosophers generally aren't known for their great listening skills. They are not remembered for the things that they heard but rather the things that they said.

Listening is a challenge. We tell our children to listen. We tell our pets to listen. We tell our spouse to listen. And then once we start to mature and begin to understand how to listen, God plays a cruel joke on us and we lose our hearing! Regardless of age, time, and location, listening is difficult. The challenge of listening is something that unites us all. No wonder that many sitcom episodes have been based on a character's inability to listen.

The problem is, even the most contemplative people among us tend to be better at speaking than listening. I don't know about you, but I find myself falling into the following scenario quite frequently. I'm having a conversation with some-one. They say something and it triggers something else in my mind. I realize that my contribution to the conversation would be so great, so profound, that I must say it. But I don't want to be too abrupt, so I wait. While I wait, I think about how I could phrase my great contribution. Like a boy who stands in front of the mirror practicing the way that he will greet a girl, I rehearse and rework what it is that I want to say. Finally, there is a pause in the conversation. My moment has arrived. The problem is, the thing that I wanted to say is no longer relevant. Unbeknownst to me, the conversation has turned to another topic. So, I zero-in on the new topic and begin to think of what I could contribute. Then it comes to me. Ah ha! I have something to say. How should I phrase it so that everyone knows I am an expert… Then once, again I get lost in my own head.

Some of us struggle with listening more than others, but Scripture conveys that this has always been a problem. James writes, "Know this, my beloved brothers: let every person be quick to hear, slow to speak, slow to anger" (James 1.19). Some have called James the wisdom writer of the New Tes-tament. Much of what he has to say sounds quite similar to Proverbs. So, we shouldn't be surprised that Proverbs has much to say about the tongue. The wisdom of Proverbs fre-quently references the importance of choosing words careful-ly (Prov 10.19; 13.3; 15.2; 17.27; 18.13, 21; 21.23). Especially helpful is Proverbs 18.13. "If one gives an answer before he hears, it is his folly and shame."

You might be wondering what this has to do with reading the Bible. Well, simply put, we bring our listening problem to our reading of Scripture. When we read Scripture, especially when we read with others, we tend to become quick to speak and slow to hear. We immediately start speaking rather than listening. We want to put in our two-cents rather than listening to what God has to say.

I have frequently heard people confess that God speaks to us in Scripture. Are we listening? If we truly believe that God is speaking through these words, then we need to actually take the time to listen. If God is continuing to breathe life into us through these words, then I need to allow some time for that to occur. I need to slow down and let God breathe into me through these words.

We were all probably taught that it is rude to interrupt when someone else is speaking. Yet that is exactly what we do when we do not take time to listen to Scripture. Typically, when we read Scripture, we immediately want to talk. We begin talking about the meaning of the text for the original audience. Then, once we think we've gotten that figured out, we start talking about what it means today. Then, we start talking to others, telling them what it means. In most books on studying the Bible, this is referred to as the stage of interpretation. It is what we do after we read. We interpret. But the way that "interpretation" is often done, it might be better to call it the stage of interruption. This is the stage where we often fail to recognize that these words are living, active, and God-breathed. Furthermore, this is the stage where we often fail to recognize that these words are worthy of meditation. Are we interpreting or interrupting? Have we really taken the time to listen, or, as the wisdom writer of Proverbs warned, have we given an answer before we have heard?

There is a story in the Old Testament that I think can provide us with an interesting way of thinking about listening to God in Scripture. It's the story of God coming to Samuel. In 1 Samuel 3, the word of God comes to Samuel, but Samuel thinks that it is Eli who is speaking. After this happens three times, Eli tells Samuel how to respond. Eli instructs Samuel to say, "Speak, LORD, for Your servant is listening" (1 Sam 3.9). The next time the word of God came to Samuel, he said, "Speak, for Your servant is listening" (1 Sam 3.10).

This ought to be the way that we approach reading Scripture. As important as maps, commentaries, and a notebook might be, acknowledging that God is speaking is even more important. Our posture is more important than our pen and paper on which we take notes. Our attitude is more important than our study aides. Speak, your servant is listening.

Why did Samuel fail to recognize God's voice? The story says that it is because he did not yet know God, and the word of God had not yet been revealed to him (1 Sam 3.7). We know that Samuel was involved in God's service (1 Sam 2.18, 26), yet despite this, he did not recognize the voice of God.

If, for a moment, we can step out of the world of 1 Samuel and back into our contemporary world, perhaps we can realize that it is possible for us to be involved in God's service and yet not recognize the word of God when it comes to us. It is possible for us to be busy with religious activities and fail to discern what God would have us to know and to be.

Furthermore, as we thought about when looking at Hebrews 4.12, perhaps the availability of Scripture has created a situation in which we fail to really listen. Scripture is on bumper stickers, refrigerator magnets, business cards, t-shirts, and so on. If we never hear the words of God, we won't recognize them, but I wonder if it could be that if we constantly surround ourselves with the words, the words can begin to lose their sacredness. If someone is speaking all the time, we eventually learn to ignore him or her. Don't misunderstand. I think it is good to surround ourselves with Scripture. But there is the possibility that we can make Scripture so commonplace that we lose our ability to listen.

If these words are living and active, then they have something to say to us. Are we "quick to hear and slow to speak" or are we so anxious to teach others, impress others, and condemn others that we will give an answer before we hear? To do so, according to Proverbs, is folly and shame.

Decreasing Distractions

"But Martha was distracted with much serving." Luke 10.40

We live in a time when there is a constant competition for our attention. Just think about driving. The job of the driver is to pay attention to the road. Yet we know that there are many crashes every day because something else is vying for the driver's attention. People have had wrecks because they have been reading billboards. Cars have crashed because someone was talking on the phone. Vehicles have slammed into each other as a result of texting. There have been accidents because people are shaving or putting on their make-up or drinking their coffee or reaching in the backseat or reading a book. And that is just while we are driving. Once we get to our destination, the distractions continue to attack us from all sides as if we are at war with the world of distractions.

I initially was going to title this chapter "Getting Rid of Distractions." But I soon came to the realization that in our times it is nearly impossible to rid oneself of distractions. The best that we can hope to do is to decrease distractions.

The problem of distractions is nothing new. Distractions come at us in new forms, but people have always faced distractions. One biblical story in particular can serve as an example. It's found in Luke 10.38–42.

> *Now as they went on their way, Jesus entered a village. And a woman named Martha welcomed him into her house. And she had a sister called Mary, who sat at the LORD's feet and listened to his teaching. But Martha was distracted with much serving. And she went up to him and said, "Lord, do you not care that my sister has left me to serve alone? Tell her then to help me." But the Lord answered her, "Martha, Martha, you are anxious and troubled about many things, but one thing is necessary. Mary has chosen the good portion, which will not be taken away from her."*

Martha was a worker. She was busy. I can see Martha cleaning the house and picking up before everyone came over. She's mopping, she's vacuuming, she's dusting the TV. She's putting the roast in the oven. She's seasoning the green beans. She's getting out the fine china.

And Mary is probably in a corner reading a book. She occasionally peaks over the pages to tell Martha that she missed a spot or that it's time to take something out of the oven. You know how siblings can be.

Then Jesus arrives at the house. When he enters, perhaps he can smell the sumptuous feast before him. Martha is rushing around. You can hear the pitter-patter of her little feet throughout the house as she goes from here to there, making sure everyone is taken care of. She might not even sit down to eat. We all know hostesses like that.

And then there's Mary. Still sitting around. Seemingly, not doing much of anything but listening to the conversation. Martha has had enough. So, those feet that were busy serving now march over to Jesus and she says, "Lord, do you not care that my sister has left me to serve alone? Tell her then to help me" (Lk 10.40). Tell her to get up off her lazy behind and get in here in the kitchen. Pour a drink, wash a dish, do something!

Jesus, then, says these surprising words. "Martha, Martha, you are anxious and troubled about many things, but one thing is necessary. Mary has chosen the good portion, which will not be taken away from her" (Lk 10.41–42). I imagine Martha's mouth fell open in utter shock. "I'm the one doing all the work and yet I'm the one being rebuked?" she may have asked herself.

This is an especially surprising story when we realize where this story falls within the Gospel of Luke. It comes right after the story of the Good Samaritan. The story of the Good Samaritan would seem to be a story about serving others. It is a story about being willing to get your hands dirty to help somebody else. It is a story about using your resources to serve others. Martha seems to be embodying the story of the Good Samaritan. The last thing that Jesus said in the Gospel of Luke after telling that parable is "You go, and do likewise" (Lk 10.37). Well, that seems to be what Martha has done. She's helping. Yet the next words out of the mouth of Jesus are, "Martha, Martha, you are anxious and troubled…" (Lk 10.41).

What has Martha done wrong? Is it wrong to be a hard worker? Is it wrong to be a servant? Is it wrong to be hospitable? To be frank, this seems like a rather confusing story. Mary gets praised for sitting down and Martha gets chastised for waiting on Jesus.

But the answer lies in what Mary was doing while she was sitting down. She was listening to the teachings of Jesus (Lk 10.39). Martha was so busy with everything else that she forgot the "one thing" (Lk 10.42) that really mattered—spending time with Jesus and his words. Mary realized what was important. She had "chosen the good portion" (Lk 10.42). There were probably lots of portions on the table. Martha had served up many portions of food. But there was only one portion that mattered. That portion was the teachings of Jesus.

Martha probably went to a lot of trouble to wait on Jesus. But the twist in this story is that the words of Jesus are the true feast. He has living water that quenches our thirst (Jn 4.14). He is the bread of life who satisfies our hunger (Jn 6.35). His words are spirit and life (Jn 6.63). When we open Scripture, these are the words before us.

Martha was missing out on these life giving words because she was distracted with less important things. How often are we like Martha? Do we fail to spend time with the words of Jesus because we are distracted? We rush, rush, rush, and perhaps fail to realize the importance of listening to Jesus' words. We all must intentionally decrease the distractions in our lives. How that is done will depend on the individual, but if we are truly going to encounter God in Scripture, we have to find a way to combat the things that compete for our attention.

Even Jesus needed to get away from the distractions. Throughout the Gospels, we are told about times that Jesus went off by himself. In the Gospel of Matthew, Jesus spends time in solitude on several occasions. After Jesus heard of the death of John the Baptist, "he withdrew from there in a boat to a desolate place by himself" (Matt 14.13). After feeding the 5000, Jesus "went up on the mountain by himself to pray" (Matt 14.23). Before the events leading up to the crucifixion, Jesus went "to a place called Gethsemane, and he said to his disciples, 'Sit here, while I go over there and pray'" (Matt 26.36). In the Gospel of Mark, early in his ministry, Jesus got up early in the morning and "went out to a desolate place, and there he prayed" (Mk 1.35). Throughout the Gospel of Luke, Jesus makes an effort to be alone. "And when it was day, he departed and went into a desolate place" (Lk 4.42). Luke makes it sound like this was a regular occurrence by noting that the crowds sought Jesus, "But he would withdraw to desolate places to pray" (Lk 5.16). Before choosing the twelve apostles, Jesus "went out to the mountain to pray, and all night he continued in prayer to God" (Lk 6.12). In the Gospel of John, when the people want to make Jesus a king, he "withdrew again to the mountain by himself" (Jn 6.15).

Jesus knew that time alone with the Father is necessary. Without it, we become run down and exhausted. We might not be able to spend all night on the mountain in prayer, but we can become more intentional about decreasing the distractions in life.

Start giving some thought to how you can decrease the distractions. I believe that we will find that listening to God becomes much easier when we learn to quiet all the other voices that are screaming for our attention. We are anxious and troubled about many things, but only one thing is necessary.

When God Speaks

"And God said, 'Let there be light,' and there was light." Genesis 1.3

There is nothing that can stand in the way of God's creative ability. Nothing challenges Him or seeks to overthrow Him. His power is simply too much. When God says, "Let there be light," we are simply told that there was light (Gen 1.3).

God speaks creation into existence. In the first chapter of the Bible, we find the phrase "God said" ten times (Gen 1.3, 6, 9, 11, 14, 20, 24, 26, 28, 29). With only a word, God creates light which penetrates the darkness. With only a word, God separates the waters. With only a word, God gathers together the billowing seas. With only a word, fruits and vegetables come forth from the earth.

With the foundation in place, God then begins to fill it. With a word, lights are placed in the heavens. With a word, living creatures inhabit the waters and the birds soar above the earth. With a word, the beasts, livestock, and swarming things roam the earth. Then God makes man and woman in His image. In the midst of all of this creating, God does something marvelous. God speaks to that which has been created. This God who is so far above us, this God whose ways we cannot fathom, this God whom we struggle to address…this God addresses us.

The book of Genesis sets the stage for the rest of Scripture. It is in Genesis that we come to understand the plight of creation and how we got in the mess that we are in. It is also in Genesis that we begin to receive hints of where this story is going. Yet we should also realize that it is in Genesis where God speaks to humankind.

God did not have to talk to creation. He could have stood back and just watched them. It could have been like the first reality TV show. He could have just observed them and I imagine it would have been quite entertaining to watch Adam and Eve try to figure out the ins and outs of life. I suppose there probably would have been some arguments between Adam and Eve that would make for good TV.

But God did not create us for His entertainment. We were not created to be God's little playthings. We were created for relationship. It's as if the love that exists between Father, Son, and Spirit cannot be contained. It must be shared. God creates male and female in His image. Furthermore, they are made king over creation as dominion is placed in their hands. They are valued and blessed. This is a good God who cares about creation.

So, as evidence of God's love, God speaks to them. We oftentimes interpret distance as disregard. That is, if there is no line of communication between two people, then a relationship does not exist. Perhaps we have been on the receiving, or giving, end of what we call the "silent treatment." The walls are up. No one is speaking. This is not a sign that the relationship is good. But God does not remain silent in this story. When God speaks to Adam and Eve, He is inviting them into a relationship. Without communication, there is not a relationship.

Although there were periods in the Old Testament when "the word of the Lord was rare" (1 Sam 3.1), God continued to speak through the prophets. Then, in the New Testament, the word became flesh (Jn 1.14). Thus, the writer of Hebrews can say that "in these last days" God has spoken to us through His Son (Heb 1.2). This God, the God of creation (Jn 1.1; Heb 1.2), dwelt among the creatures. He ate. He slept. He cried. He lived. He lived a life like the rest of us yet without sin (Heb 4.15).

They called Him Immanuel, God with us (Matt 1.23). When Jesus spoke, God was speaking. It was not a word from a far-away, distant land. But rather, God entered into people's homes, professions, and places of worship. He spoke to them.

One of the most controversial aspects of Christianity is the notion that God lived in the flesh among creation. We struggle to articulate how Jesus could be divine and human. We wrestle with understanding how God could be God and yet also very close. Yet this belief, as difficult as it might be, is crucial to our understanding of Scripture.

God's closeness to creation did not cease when Jesus ascended. In a very real sense, Christ continues to live with us. He continues to inhabit our homes, our professions, and our places of worship. To the extent that His words are living *within* us, He is living *among* us.

Let that sink in for a moment. Christ is still living with us insofar as His words are active among us. He told the disciples that they would not be left alone. When He left, He said that

He would send "another Helper" (Jn 14.16). The Spirit was sent to be a helper and comforter, a teacher, one who would stir up memories, and one who convicts (Jn 14.16; 16.8). The Spirit was these things to the disciples, but I believe the Spirit is also these things to us. One of the ways that this is accomplished is through the church's Scripture.

The apostles were not left alone. But neither are we. God continues to speak. He speaks most clearly and profoundly through the words that have been written. In the beginning, God said. And when "he said," new possibilities were created. His words were life giving. New realities were breathed into existence.

God's words continue to give life. Our sacred Scriptures are a source of creation and of newness. When we submit to the gospel contained therein, we become new (2 Corinthians 5.17). God creates order from the chaos of our lives. He creates light where there was darkness. With His words, God does in us what He did at creation. He creates something new.

When we open the Bible, we should be in awe. We should be in awe that God has chosen to speak.

The Holy Spirit and Life

"And I will give you a new heart, and a new spirit I will put within you. And I will remove the heart of stone from your flesh and give you a heart of flesh. And I will put my Spirit within you, and cause you to walk in my statutes and be careful to obey my rules." Ezekiel 35.26–27

No understanding of Scripture is complete without giving adequate thought to the Holy Spirit. After all, the church confesses that the Spirit is behind the writing and preservation of these sacred texts (Heb 3.7, 10.15–17; 1 Pet 1.10–12). We often think of the Spirit as the one who inspired Scriptures and performed miracles. For many, that is the extent of the Spirit's work.

I can vividly recall being in Bible class in the little, musty room of the old country church. May God bless those who teach our youth, for you never know where the discussion might go. On one occasion, the conversation went to the Holy Spirit. The teacher was asked to explain what the Holy Spirit is doing today. After thinking for a moment, he replied with something to the extent of, "Well, nothing." I don't fault him entirely. This is the thinking that many of us were brought up with. Just as Christ completed His work and sat down at the right hand of the Father, so too, in the minds of many, the Spirit completed His work and sat down after some miracles were performed and John wrote the final "Amen" to conclude the book of Revelation.

Sadly, this is simply not in accord with what is found in Scripture. One passage that makes this clear is Romans 8.26–27. "Likewise the Spirit helps us in our weakness. For we do not know what to pray for as we ought, but the Spirit himself intercedes for us with groanings too deep for words. And he who searches hearts knows what is the mind of the Spirit, because the Spirit intercedes for the saints according to the will of God."

The interpretation that the Spirit is doing "Well, nothing" is not unique to one group of churches. Although things are gradually beginning to change, you will find few churches on American soil that have given much attention to the Spirit over the last couple of centuries. I might also add that the African-American churches have historically given more thought to the Spirit than have churches made up of Caucasian members.

What might explain this void? There are at least a couple of reasons for the neglect of the Spirit. For starters, most Westerners have been conditioned to prefer that things be verifiable and provable. The period known as the Enlightenment created an environment where everything had to be rationally explained with the five senses. So, in many circles, discussions of the Spirit began to wane. Perhaps the Spirit is just a bit too mysterious for our modern sensibilities. (Many people will instinctively cringe a little at the word "mysterious." This is my point exactly!) Second, as educated Americans we like to think that we are self-sufficient. The biblical notion of the Spirit runs counter to our self-sufficiency. In order to accept that we need the Spirit who can help us "in our weaknesses," we must first admit that we are weak and need help. Historically speaking, it would seem that as our self-sufficiency goes up, our talk of the Spirit goes down.

In what follows, I hope to sketch a biblical portrait of the Spirit in very broad strokes. This is not an exhaustive study of the Spirit. Rather, I hope to provide a general framework through which Scriptures dealing with the Spirit can be interpreted.

Since we frequently use the word "spirit" in our speech, it would be wise to begin by defining what we mean. We speak of team spirit, Christmas spirit, high spirits, etc. There may even be a little store in your town where you can buy spirits. In Scripture, the word "Spirit" can mean breath, or wind. Both the Hebrew *(ruach)* and the Greek *(pneuma)* carry this meaning. You may recognize the Greek word because it is found in some of our medical terminology (people with *pneumonia* have a hard time *breath*ing).

Several Scriptures express the idea of the Spirit being at work with the Father and Son. Baptism was done "in the name of the *Father* and of the *Son* and of the *Holy Spirit*" (Matt 28.19 emphasis added). Thus, Paul can write, "The grace of the *Lord Jesus Christ* and the love of *God* and the fellowship of the *Holy Spirit* be with you all" (2 Cor 13.14 emphasis added). Or, as is written in Titus 3.4–6, "But when the goodness and loving kindness of *God our Savior* appeared, he saved us, not because of works done by us in righteousness, but according to his own mercy, by the washing of regeneration and renewal of the *Holy Spirit*, whom he poured out on us richly through *Jesus Christ our Savior*" (emphasis added).

As we try to sketch what the Spirit is up to, it is helpful to note that in the Old Testament, God's Spirit is associated with creation and life. Remember, Spirit is breath. The Spirit must be present for there to be life and light. In Genesis 1.2, "the Spirit of God was hovering over the face of the waters." In order for Adam to live, "the breath of life" must be "breathed into" him (Gen 2.7). Reflecting on all that God has made, Psalm 104.30 declares, "When you send forth your Spirit, they are created, and you renew the face of the ground." Similarly "the breath of his mouth" is necessary for creation (Ps 33.6). Without the Spirit of God, humankind cannot live (Gen 6.3; 7.22). This understanding of God's Spirit is also found in Job 27.2–4, 32.8, 33.4, and 34.13–15. Where God's Spirit is, God is (Ps 139.7).

In the Old Testament, the Spirit of God is a life-giver. Where the Spirit is, there is life. Where the Spirit is not, there is death. Without this foundation, we can't really begin to understand the work of the Spirit in the New Testament. I think much of the misunderstanding and avoidance of the Spirit stems from a lack of having this basic framework in place. We want to skip to the New Testament. But we have to understand the Newer Testament in light of the Older Testament.

The prophets anticipated a time when all of God's people would have true life in the Spirit. There is a good example of this in Ezekiel. "I will sprinkle clean water on you, and you shall be clean from all your uncleannesses, and from all your idols I will cleanse you. And I will give you a new heart, and a new spirit I will put within you. And I will remove the heart of stone from your flesh and give you a heart of flesh. *And I will put my Spirit within you*, and cause you to walk in my statutes and be careful to obey my rules" (Ezek 36.25–27 emphasis added). There is an expectation of new life for the people of God, but in order for this to occur, God's Spirit must be within them.

This new life has its origins in Christ. He is now the source of new life (Rom 6.11) and new creation (2 Cor 5.17) for the people of God. He promised that upon his departure the people of God would not be left alone. Jesus told the disciples, "And I will ask the Father, and he will give you another Helper, to be with you forever" (Jn 14.16). The Spirit, therefore, can be thought of as the presence of Christ in Christ's physical absence. This is why Paul uses phrases like "the Spirit of Christ" (Rom 8.9), "the Spirit of his Son" (Gal 4.6), and "the Spirit of Jesus Christ" (Phil 1.19).

With the coming of Christ, entry into the people of God is open to all. When one is baptized, God's Spirit is placed within the new creature (Acts 2.38). When read within an Old Testament backdrop (along with Paul's teaching about death, life, and baptism in Romans 6) Acts 2.38 seems pretty clear. Just as the breath of life had to be breathed into Adam in order for him to become a living creature, without the Spirit, we are dead. The Spirit connects us to Christ who makes it possible for us to have union with the Father. We have come out of the darkness and into the light. We have joined the story of God's redemption. As is promised in Ezekiel, God's Spirit is within us and we are newly alive. We partner with the Spirit as we try to live this new life, individually and collectively.

This is the contrast that Paul makes between flesh and Spirit. Where the Spirit of God is, there is life. Where the

Spirit of God is not, there is death. Therefore, Paul can refer to the Spirit as "the Spirit of life" (Rom 8.2), he can say that "the Spirit is life" (Rom 8.10), and he can say "by the Spirit... you will live" (Rom 8.13). Similarly, in Galatians, Christians "live by the Spirit" (Gal 5.25).

When God's life-giving Spirit is within us, things are made new. Where there was hatred there is love (Rom 5.5), where there was despair there is joy (1 Thess 1.6), where there was discord there is peace (Rom 14.17), and through the power of the Holy Spirit we have hope (Rom 15.13).

Part Two

Part Two Introduction

In what follows, I hope to propose a way that we can read Scripture devotionally. It is not intended to replace that which we might think of as studying the text. It is also not meant to replace reading the Scriptures with others. I simply wish to re-introduce us to a way of reading Scripture that has largely fallen out of favor in many of our churches.

I'm going to suggest that we approach a devotional reading with 4 Rs: reflect, read, respond, and rest.

Reflect

Reflect on your day or what is going on in your life. On the upcoming pages that have been provided, you have a category called ups and a category called downs. Before you begin your devotional reading, take a few minutes to think about the emotions you've experienced during the day (if you're doing this in the evening), or what you've experienced the day before (if you're doing this in the morning). When did you feel close to God and when did you feel far away? When did you feel like you were moving toward faith, hope, and love, and when did you feel like you were moving away from those things?

There are a few reasons for doing this. First, it is a practice in self-awareness. If you try to make a habit of taking note of what you have felt and why you have felt it, it becomes much easier to process and understand these emotions rather than going to unhealthy extremes. One extreme is holding everything in. The other extreme is releasing whatever you are feeling on the closest person. Neither is very helpful for anyone involved.

Second, by reflecting on our day we are taking a moment to realize the areas in our lives where God may want to say something to us. Psalm 119.143 says, "Trouble and anguish have found me out, but your commandments are my delight."

Third, taking some time to reflect on the day helps us to clear our head. Just the act of writing something down can help us make sense of things. We are preparing ourselves to enter into the presence of God by opening the Scriptures. Try to do this with a mind that is centered and at ease.

So, before we begin reading, we'll take a few minutes to reflect on what's going on around us and within us, trusting that God will have something to say to us. Doing this on a regular basis helps us to become more self-aware, it helps us to recognize the places in our lives that need to be restored with Scripture, and it helps us to clear our minds so that we can really engage God in the reading.

Read

Once we've taken a few minutes to reflect, we're now going to read. You will find 52 readings on the pages that follow. This is meant to be done weekly, but feel free to make it flexible to your schedule. I've chosen the Psalms and the Gospel of Mark. By no means is a devotional reading of Scripture limited to these portions of the Bible, but historically the Psalms and the Gospels have provided many Christians with devotional readings. Certain portions of text just lend themselves more toward a devotional approach.

Reading devotionally will be very different, and perhaps even awkward, for some of us. This is a type of reading that is not concerned with following cross-references. If you have a study Bible, I would encourage you not to use it for your devotional reading. They have their place, but with this type of reading, we are not concerned with timelines and archaeological discoveries. With the devotional reading of Scripture, we are hoping to hear a word from God. God can speak even if we don't know when a book of the Bible was written, where some of the events took place, or who the world rulers were at the time.

Read the passage slowly a couple of times. Notice which words, phrases, or ideas stand out to you. Don't overthink this. This is where we trust that the Author is with us. Something will likely jump off of the page. If not, that's ok. It doesn't always happen. But, more times than not, something will leap out and smack you upside the head. (From a theological perspective, I believe this is one of the works of the Holy Spirit today. The Spirit smacks us upside the head with what we need.)

As an example, this morning I read Matthew 8.18–22 devotionally. This is where a scribe comes and wants to follow Jesus and Jesus says, "Foxes have holes, and birds of the air have nests, but the Son of Man has nowhere to lay his head" (Matt 8.20). The phrase, "the Son of Man has nowhere to lay his head," stayed with me. I found comfort in the notion that Jesus did not chase after possessions but rather knew that God would provide.

There is a time to do research on the role that the Scribe plays in the Gospel of Matthew, why it is that Jesus chose the example of the fox and the bird and what we know about these creatures, where this portion of Scripture falls within the larger framework of Matthew, etc. But that's not what we're concerned with when we read devotionally. When we read devotionally, we trust that God will say something pertinent to us regardless of whether or not we are Gospel of Matthew scholars.

Once you believe you have discerned the word, phrase, or idea that God would have you to know, spend some time with it. You may just sit for a few minutes and let those words cover you. Allow those words to be alive. Let them seep into dark corners and bring light. Think about your reflection on your day. What would God have you to know or to be? What is being spoken to you?

Respond

We trust that God speaks in Scripture. We also ought to use Scripture as a starting point for us to speak to God. Having received a word from God through Scripture, what would you like to say to God? This is the portion of the devotional reading when we respond. This response might be a lengthy prayer or it might be, "Thank you" or "Forgive me."

In this way, the devotional reading of Scripture becomes a dialogue of sorts. Scripture serves as a conversation starter. We trust that God speaks to us and then we respond to God.

Rest

Having heard from God in Scripture, and having responded, take some time to rest in God's presence. There are 24 hours in a day. If we can't comfortable sit still before God for 5 minutes, it really ought to make us wonder where we are spiritually. You might think, "I have so much to do." But, I think you will find that if you incorporate this way of reading Scripture—reflect, read, respond, rest—you will find that the day becomes quite a bit smoother.

I realize that this way of reading isn't for everybody. For some, it probably even seems a bit cheesy. That's ok. I simply ask that you be open to the approach. There are many who will benefit from this type of reading. It's not a reading that denies the necessity of scholarly work. Rather, it is a reading that acknowledges that there are times when all of my books and all of my learning might be getting in the way of letting God say what He wants to say to me.

I hope that this way of reading can become a way of life for you. On the pages that follow you'll find 52 Scriptures. Some days we will read a Psalm and some days we will read a portion of the Gospel of Mark. Just to be clear, we aren't studying the Psalms or studying Mark. We are reading portions of the Psalms and portions of Mark devotionally, expecting that God will have something to say to us. You'll notice that the readings are short. This is intentional. The aim is not to cover a lot of Scripture. The aim is to allow a little bit of Scripture to cover us.

I haven't provided the text on the page for a couple of reasons. One reason is so that you can read it using whatever translation and whatever medium you prefer. Another reason I haven't provided the text itself is because I believe opening up the Bible (or, if you must, your Bible app) is part of the process of a devotional reading. There should be an acknowledgement that we are coming in contact with the Sacred.

The goal is to try to do this once a week. What I have provided is a simple template to help you get started. This is just one approach. Feel free to change it after you have done it for a while. It also might be helpful if you go back and review every few weeks to see where you have been on this journey. Ultimately, I hope that we can create a space in our lives to hear the Holy.

Daily Workbook

Reflect
My Ups:

My Downs:

Read Psalm 1
My Word, Phrase, or Idea:

Respond to God
My Prayer:

Rest in God's Presence

Reflect
My Ups:

My Downs:

Read Mark 1.4–8
My Word, Phrase, or Idea:

Respond to God
My Prayer:

Rest in God's Presence

Reflect
My Ups:

My Downs:

Read Psalm 15
My Word, Phrase, or Idea:

Respond to God
My Prayer:

Rest in God's Presence

Reflect
My Ups:

My Downs:

Read Mark 1.9–14
My Word, Phrase, or Idea:

Respond to God
My Prayer:

Rest in God's Presence

Reflect
My Ups:

My Downs:

Read Psalm 23
My Word, Phrase, or Idea:

Respond to God
My Prayer:

Rest in God's Presence

Reflect
My Ups:

My Downs:

Read Mark 1.16–20
My Word, Phrase, or Idea:

Respond to God
My Prayer:

Rest in God's Presence

Reflect
My Ups:

My Downs:

Read Psalm 43
My Word, Phrase, or Idea:

Respond to God
My Prayer:

Rest in God's Presence

Reflect
My Ups:

My Downs:

Read Mark 1.35–39
My Word, Phrase, or Idea:

Respond to God
My Prayer:

Rest in God's Presence

Reflect

My Ups:

My Downs:

Read Psalm 53

My Word, Phrase, or Idea:

Respond to God

My Prayer:

Rest in God's Presence

Reflect

My Ups:

My Downs:

Read Mark 2.13–17

My Word, Phrase, or Idea:

Respond to God

My Prayer:

Rest in God's Presence

Reflect
My Ups:

My Downs:

Read Psalm 54
My Word, Phrase, or Idea:

Respond to God
My Prayer:

Rest in God's Presence

Reflect
My Ups:

My Downs:

Read Mark 3.7–12
My Word, Phrase, or Idea:

Respond to God
My Prayer:

Rest in God's Presence

Reflect
My Ups:

My Downs:

Read Psalm 67
My Word, Phrase, or Idea:

Respond to God
My Prayer:

Rest in God's Presence

Reflect

My Ups:

My Downs:

Read Mark 3.31–35

My Word, Phrase, or Idea:

Respond to God

My Prayer:

Rest in God's Presence

Reflect
My Ups:

My Downs:

Read Psalm 70
My Word, Phrase, or Idea:

Respond to God
My Prayer:

Rest in God's Presence

Reflect
My Ups:

My Downs:

Read Mark 4.21–25
My Word, Phrase, or Idea:

Respond to God
My Prayer:

Rest in God's Presence

Reflect
My Ups:

My Downs:

Read Psalm 87
My Word, Phrase, or Idea:

Respond to God
My Prayer:

Rest in God's Presence

Reflect
My Ups:

My Downs:

Read Mark 4.30–32
My Word, Phrase, or Idea:

Respond to God
My Prayer:

Rest in God's Presence

Reflect

My Ups:

My Downs:

Read Psalm 93

My Word, Phrase, or Idea:

Respond to God

My Prayer:

Rest in God's Presence

Reflect
My Ups:

My Downs:

Read Mark 4.35–41
My Word, Phrase, or Idea:

Respond to God
My Prayer:

Rest in God's Presence

Reflect
My Ups:

My Downs:

Read Psalm 100
My Word, Phrase, or Idea:

Respond to God
My Prayer:

Rest in God's Presence

Reflect
My Ups:

My Downs:

Read Mark 6.1–6
My Word, Phrase, or Idea:

Respond to God
My Prayer:

Rest in God's Presence

Reflect
My Ups:

My Downs:

Read Psalm 110
My Word, Phrase, or Idea:

Respond to God
My Prayer:

Rest in God's Presence

Reflect
My Ups:

My Downs:

Read Mark 6.53–56
My Word, Phrase, or Idea:

Respond to God
My Prayer:

Rest in God's Presence

Reflect
My Ups:

My Downs:

Read Psalm 117
My Word, Phrase, or Idea:

Respond to God
My Prayer:

Rest in God's Presence

Reflect

My Ups:

My Downs:

Read Mark 8.34–38

My Word, Phrase, or Idea:

Respond to God

My Prayer:

Rest in God's Presence

Reflect

My Ups:

My Downs:

Read Psalm 119.25–32

My Word, Phrase, or Idea:

Respond to God

My Prayer:

Rest in God's Presence

Reflect

My Ups:

My Downs:

Read Mark 9.2–8

My Word, Phrase, or Idea:

Respond to God

My Prayer:

Rest in God's Presence

Reflect
My Ups:

My Downs:

Read Psalm 119.57–64
My Word, Phrase, or Idea:

Respond to God
My Prayer:

Rest in God's Presence

Reflect
My Ups:

My Downs:

Read Mark 9.38–41
My Word, Phrase, or Idea:

Respond to God
My Prayer:

Rest in God's Presence

Reflect
My Ups:

My Downs:

Read Psalm 119.97–104
My Word, Phrase, or Idea:

Respond to God
My Prayer:

Rest in God's Presence

Reflect
My Ups:

My Downs:

Read Mark 10.13–16
My Word, Phrase, or Idea:

Respond to God
My Prayer:

Rest in God's Presence

Reflect
My Ups:

My Downs:

Read Psalm 119.129–136
My Word, Phrase, or Idea:

Respond to God
My Prayer:

Rest in God's Presence

Reflect
My Ups:

My Downs:

Read Mark 12.28–34
My Word, Phrase, or Idea:

Respond to God
My Prayer:

Rest in God's Presence

Reflect
My Ups:

My Downs:

Read Psalm 120
My Word, Phrase, or Idea:

Respond to God
My Prayer:

Rest in God's Presence

Reflect
My Ups:

My Downs:

Read Mark 12.41–44
My Word, Phrase, or Idea:

Respond to God
My Prayer:

Rest in God's Presence

Reflect
My Ups:

My Downs:

Read Psalm 123
My Word, Phrase, or Idea:

Respond to God
My Prayer:

Rest in God's Presence

Reflect

My Ups:

My Downs:

Read Mark 14.3–9

My Word, Phrase, or Idea:

Respond to God

My Prayer:

Rest in God's Presence

Reflect
My Ups:

My Downs:

Read Psalm 125
My Word, Phrase, or Idea:

Respond to God
My Prayer:

Rest in God's Presence

Reflect
My Ups:

My Downs:

Read Mark 14.22–25
My Word, Phrase, or Idea:

Respond to God
My Prayer:

Rest in God's Presence

Reflect
My Ups:

My Downs:

Read Psalm 126
My Word, Phrase, or Idea:

Respond to God
My Prayer:

Rest in God's Presence

Reflect
My Ups:

My Downs:

Read Mark 15.1–5
My Word, Phrase, or Idea:

Respond to God
My Prayer:

Rest in God's Presence

Reflect

My Ups:

My Downs:

Read Psalm 128

My Word, Phrase, or Idea:

Respond to God

My Prayer:

Rest in God's Presence

Reflect

My Ups:

My Downs:

Read Mark 15.16–20

My Word, Phrase, or Idea:

Respond to God

My Prayer:

Rest in God's Presence

Reflect
My Ups:

My Downs:

Read Psalm 131
My Word, Phrase, or Idea:

Respond to God
My Prayer:

Rest in God's Presence

Reflect
My Ups:

My Downs:

Read Mark 15.40–41
My Word, Phrase, or Idea:

Respond to God
My Prayer:

Rest in God's Presence

Reflect
My Ups:

My Downs:

Read Psalm 134
My Word, Phrase, or Idea:

Respond to God
My Prayer:

Rest in God's Presence

Reflect
My Ups:

My Downs:

Read Mark 15.42–47
My Word, Phrase, or Idea:

Respond to God
My Prayer:

Rest in God's Presence

Reflect
My Ups:

My Downs:

Read Psalm 142
My Word, Phrase, or Idea:

Respond to God
My Prayer:

Rest in God's Presence

Reflect
My Ups:

My Downs:

Read Mark 16.1–8
My Word, Phrase, or Idea:

Respond to God
My Prayer:

Rest in God's Presence

Reflect
My Ups:

My Downs:

Read Psalm 150
My Word, Phrase, or Idea:

Respond to God
My Prayer:

Rest in God's Presence

Reflect
My Ups:

My Downs:

Read Mark 16.19–20
My Word, Phrase, or Idea:

Respond to God
My Prayer:

Rest in God's Presence

For a full listing of our books, visit DeWard's website:

www.deward.com

DeWard™

for your journey